The Personal Freedom Book

Edward Phelps

1st Edition

Published by PocketAwareness™

Print/Paperback ISBN: 978-1-944718-10-7
Downloadable Audio ISBN: 978-1-944718-09-1
Digital Online ISBN: 978-1-944718-11-4

Contents

Your Free Bonus Chapter Is Waiting...

Are you ready to finally stop blocking your own freedom? Learn the secret practice that unlocks your personal freedom in the special bonus chapter.

Click the link below to get your free copy:

thepersonalfreedombook.com/free-bonus-chapter

Acknowledgments

To my Mom, I love you!

To my beautiful and talented daughters, may your journey's be full with love (it's all you need).

And to my friends and enemies who have all contributed to the rich fabric that is my life... thank you!

Foreward

"Where the mind is without fear and the head is
held high;

Where knowledge is free;

Where the world has not been broken up into
fragments by narrow domestic walls;

Where words come out from the depth of truth;

Where tireless striving stretches its arms
towards perfection;

Where the clear stream of reason has not lost its
way into the dreary desert sand of dead habit;

Where the mind is led forward by thee into ever-
widening thought and action—

Into that heaven of freedom, my Father, let my
country awake."

~ **Rabindranath Tagore**
From his seminal work: Gitanjali

Chapter 1

In The Beginning

From the moment we are born we are given a bunch of ideas about the world that we use for the rest of our lives. We do not choose these ideas for ourselves; they are given to us by our parents and family, at church and at school. They are forced upon us when we are infants, before we are able to fully understand and choose for ourselves. This is important if we are concerned about our freedom because everything we think, do, and feel we can do, is based upon these ideas we did not choose for ourselves.

These ideas tell us about our world. Let's call these ideas we are given about the world 'core beliefs' because we use them as the foundation for how we look at the world, and we believe in them intensely. Every day we are free to make choices that direct the course of our lives, and we make all those choices based upon our core beliefs. We build our lives on our core beliefs. Our core beliefs include our ideas about the most basic things like what are good, bad, right, and wrong. Other core beliefs include our thoughts about gender (male or female), parents (mom and dad), family (sisters, brothers, aunts, uncles and cousins), community (nationality, race, class), religion (where we come from, God, good and evil), and so much more.

Don Miguel Ruiz describes our core beliefs as 'agreements' in his timeless book 'The Four Agreements.' This is a really effective way of describing the concept of what beliefs actually are (agreements). We lock-in our core beliefs, our foundation agreements, at a very young age and then go through our entire lives without ever questioning or changing them. Everything in our lives constantly changes, except our core beliefs. Bottom line, we never review our core beliefs to see how they are working for us.

In this book we will examine how deeply our core beliefs (foundation agreements) affect our freedom, what freedom really is and how to have more of it. We will also examine the awesome power of choice and how our choices affect our freedom.

Notes:

Before we can start exploring to improve or better understand ourselves and our place in the world we must first be aware that we live our lives under the power of deep core agreements that we did not choose.

These core agreements, or core beliefs, tell us how we look at ourselves, other people, situations and circumstances we encounter, and the world. They decide what we feel is acceptable, and even possible. They are extremely powerful beliefs that we live by, and did not choose for ourselves.

Review Chapter 1

Take the chapter review quiz.

Quiz 1.1 - In The Beginning

Question 1 of 3

What is forced upon you when you are a child that tells you how you see the world?

A. Your Parents

B. Your Family

C. Your Core Beliefs

D. Your Life

Question 2 of 3

Where do core beliefs come from?

A. Parents

B. Family

C. Community

D. Religion

E. School

F. All of the Above

Question 3 of 3

What changes a thought into a belief?

A. Strong Agreement

B. God

C. Everyone Else Believes It

Chapter 2

Beliefs

Have you ever thought about what a belief actually is? Probably not. Most people never do. Yet everything we do is based upon our beliefs. Beliefs are the most powerful thoughts we have. That's right, beliefs are thoughts. They are the thoughts we feel most strongly about. We think a lot of thoughts, and yet we spend very little, or no time at all, thinking about what thinking is, or how it works.

The average person has between fifty thousand (50,000) and seventy thousand (70,000) thoughts every day. That's between thirty five (35) and forty eight (48) thoughts every minute. If you think thirty five (35) thoughts every minute, you spend 58 percent (58%) of every minute thinking. That grows to spending eighty percent (80%) of every minute thinking if you think forty eight (48) thoughts every minute. That's a lot of thoughts. This constant thinking is like a really thick wall between our thoughts and our feelings, our mind and our heart. Constant thinking blocks us from seeing or listening clearly, and feeling deeply which affects our sense of freedom.

So let's look at what thoughts are. Thoughts are the things we think with our brain, and they only exist in our mind. We think different kinds of thoughts about different kinds of things. Our thoughts tell us what we like and don't like, what we want and don't want. They even tell us what is good, bad, right, and wrong. But our thoughts exist only in our mind. Nobody can read our thoughts or know what they are. We talk, write, and use sign language to tell other people what we are thinking because they can't know what we are thinking unless we tell them.

Our beliefs are thoughts that we agree with intensely, maintain, and do not change. What transforms a thought into a belief is how strong the agreement we have with that thought is. We give specific meanings, rules, and expected behaviors to our belief thoughts, and then we strongly agree with them. The strength of our agreement with our belief thoughts is so strong that we do not question or change our beliefs.

Beliefs are powerful mental tools we can use to help us be who we want, and get the things we want. Beliefs direct the course of our will and decide what and how we do what we do in life. When a belief thought is shared by a group of people it becomes even more powerful. Beliefs are so powerful that great wars are fought over them. Religions have many belief thoughts shared by large groups of people who very strongly agree with them. One group, with its own beliefs, may not agree with the beliefs of another group.

Our belief thoughts govern our lives. We do not think of our beliefs as thoughts. They are much greater than just thoughts to us. But if we go deeply into this and examine the true nature of a belief we will see that they are in fact thoughts. When we do this, we will also know that we have the power to review and even change our beliefs. We can stop holding onto chains of thought that don't work for us. We can become aware of our power over our beliefs. Reviewing our beliefs is an essential part of our personal freedom.

Notes:
We live our lives guided by our beliefs. And yet we rarely think deeply about what a belief actually is, how beliefs work, or how we can use beliefs to get what we want.

Review Chapter 2

Take the chapter review quiz.

Quiz 2.1 - Beliefs.

Question 1 of 3

A thought...?

A. Is Not Real

B. Cannot Change Anything

C. Exists Only In The Mind of the Thinker

Question 2 of 3

What changes a thought into a belief?

A. Faith

B. Strong Agreement

C. Wisdom

Question 3 of 3

What do your beliefs do for you?

A. Help You Make Decisions

B. Help You Feel Better

C. Make You Strong

Chapter 3

Freedom

"You shall be free indeed when your days are not without a care nor your nights without a want and a grief, But rather when these things girdle your life and yet you rise above them naked and unbound."

~ Kahlil Gibran

Freedom, the word, is instantly recognized as a state of existence people want in some form, at some time. We seek freedom across all areas of our lives, and we fight intensely for our state of freedom.

What Is Freedom?

Freedom is the eternal state in each moment - each instant we encounter - where choices are available. If we have a choice, then we are free. We can check on our state of freedom anytime simply by asking, 'do I have a choice?' If we explore this more deeply it becomes clear that we are always free because we always have a choice (even though we may not like the choices we have).

Seeking Freedom

Let's break down the idea of seeking freedom a bit. If we seek freedom it means we want it. If we want freedom that means we feel we do not have it. But, if we never had freedom before, we would not want it. We want freedom because we have had it before, we know how it feels, and we liked it. Wanting or seeking freedom raises a really important question. If we had freedom before, and we feel we don't have it now, then where did our freedom go?

What Takes Freedom Away?

With every choice we make, we give away some of our freedom. Our freedom in any situation is reduced from all the choices available, down to the single choice we make. Think about this. Before we make a choice we have many choices available. After we make a choice, the other choices are gone. We have removed the other choices and all the other possibilities from the situation.

So, what causes us to feel like we are not free? We don't feel like our freedom is taken away when our choices, our wants, our desires are considered. When we feel we are not free, we are actually expressing that we do not 'like' the choices available to us. Put another way, we feel we are not free when we don't have the choices we want. There are two reasons why we don't like the choices we have:

1. Because of how we look at things.
2. Because we feel the choices available are not ours.

How We Look At Things

Our beliefs decide how we look at things. They tell us what choices we feel we have. In any situation we have choices, options to choose from, but we ignore or reject the options that do not fit our beliefs. We use our beliefs to make judgements about our feelings, the people, and the conditions we are faced with. We use our beliefs to tell us which choices are acceptable, and which are not. We strongly agree with our beliefs, and with that agreement we accept the limits on our choices that come with those beliefs. Because we agree so strongly, because we believe, we do not feel these limits take away our freedom. If we are concerned with our freedom, it is helpful to recognize that whenever we make a choice we limit the options available to us, and we limit our freedom.

We feel our freedom has been taken away when the choices we have do not fit our beliefs. This feeling of not being free changes if we change our beliefs. A new belief changes the way we look at things, and helps us look at a situation in a new way. When we change how we look at a situation, different choices become acceptable that may not have been acceptable before. A simple example of this is when we choose to change a favorite sports team. The next time the new favorite team plays the old favorite team, we root for the new team. Then when a penalty happens we view the referees decision as fair or unfair based upon if it helps, or hurts, our new team. This ability to completely change how we look at things is an example of the awesome power of belief.

When The Choices Available Are Not Ours

Many times we find ourselves in situations where choices have been made, but the choices we want were not included. This happens a lot at work and in politics where laws and rules are made that we don't agree with, but we choose to honor them to avoid punishment. When this happens, when we make choices that we don't agree with, we feel our freedom has been taken away. Notice that we choose to make these choices, even though we do not agree with them. Using a workplace example where you are asked to do something by a superior or follow a rule, you might explain why you made this choice saying something like 'I have to or I will get fired.' That may be true (or it may not be true), but nothing is forcing you to make the choices you make. You are free to choose something else and deal with the consequences later. The important thing here is not to judge your choice (I should/could/would have this..., or I shouldn't/couldn't/wouldn't have that...), but instead to know and accept that you made a choice. Knowing when you make a choice gives you the freedom to make another choice later on if you want to.

Notes:

Freedom is very important to us. We want freedom in all areas of our lives. But it is the fact that we want freedom that shows we do not understand what freedom is, its awesome power, or how we can have it.

Review Chapter 3

Take the chapter review quiz.

Quiz 3.1 - Freedom.

Question 1 of 6

What is Freedom?

A. A right we are born with.

B. The ability to express yourself.

C. The ability to make a choice.

Question 2 of 6

What takes your freedom away?

A. Making Choices

B. Bad Rules and Laws

C. People With More Power

Question 3 of 6

Where do the choices you have come from?

A. The Situation

B. Your Beliefs

C. The Rules or Laws

Question 4 of 6

You must always follow a rule or law?

A. False

B. Depends C. True

Question 5 of 6

You feel like you are not free when?

A. The world is against you.

B. You don't have the choices you want.

C. Your freedom is taken away.

Question 6 of 6

How can you have more freedom?

A. Review and Change Some of Your Beliefs

B. Fight Harder

C. Pray

Chapter 4

Choice

"We can make a choice, or not.
Either way, we will have chosen."

~ Edward Phelps

Based upon our examination of freedom so far, we know that we have freedom whenever we have choices. If we look deeply into this three things about freedom become clear. First, freedom is always present. We know this because in any moment we have choices we can make. Second, every choice we make takes away some of our freedom. And third, we do not feel free when we don't like the choices we have.

What Is Choice?

Choice is the mental process where, in any moment, a single option is selected from all the options available. Choices are expressed first as thoughts (you think 'I choose this, or that...'), and then ultimately as actions (you do something based on the choice you made). Some other words used to describe choices are: preference, pick, selection, decision, option, alternative, will, and willpower.

Choices are how we move through life. Our choices determine what we think, what we believe, what we feel, and what we do. Every choice we make affects everyone and everything in our lives. For each choice we are faced with (what to do, what to feel, what to believe, what to say, etc.) we get different options to choose from.

When we make a choice in one situation, that choice creates an entirely new situation with all new choices. For example: if we are driving or walking, when we come to an intersection we have five choices available. These five choices are: go-straight, turn-around, turn- left, turn-right, or stay where we are. If we choose turn- left, the entire situation is transformed from what it was, a standing at an intersection situation, into a new turn-left situation with new choices available to us as we go down that new road to the left.

Types Of Choices

There are two types of choices:

- **Belief Choices:** Choices based upon chosen beliefs, past experience and social norms that have predictable outcomes.
- **Creative Choices:** Choices based upon inner inspiration that have unpredictable outcomes.

All the choices we make at home, at work, at play, and in our relationships are either belief choices or creative choices. No matter which type of choices we make, we are free to make them. By understanding the types of choices available we can make choices that are more likely to get us what we want or where we want to be.

Belief Choices

Belief choices are choices we make that are based on our beliefs. They promote expected behavior and outcomes.

Whenever we make belief choices we are choosing to go with what we feel we know, rather than risk having a new experience that we may not like. Belief choices support our desire for safety and control over our situations and circumstances. Making belief choices satisfies our fears when we make them, but our fears return, in new forms, soon after.

We do all we can to prevent things we like in our lives from changing. We prefer to repeat what we know and like instead of trying new things which we may not like. The majority of the choices we make are belief choices because they help us prevent changes we don't want. Examples of belief choices are:

- Feeling afraid because of how someone or something looks;
- Feeling happy (or sad) based on what someone says;
- Doing something because we feel it is 'safe'.

These are all examples of belief choices because the way we feel and the actions we take are based on what we believe. The root of these beliefs are based in some past experience that we liked. In the first example, we fear a person because of some past experience or what someone we trust told us about somebody who looks like them (or their type or kind). In the second example, without knowing the true intent of the person who spoke, we are happy (or sad) when someone speaks words that we believe have a happy (or sad) meaning. In the third example, we choose to do something because we feel safe about it, and our feeling of safety is based on some past experience we liked or a trusted recommendation.

Creative Choices

Creative choices promote our inner vision and lead to change and the creation of new things. They lead us down a creative path which creates things that have not existed in the past, do not exist now, and will only exist in the future.

The creative path is full of unknowns and questions that cannot be answered by anything we know now. Creative choices drive change in our world. Every new invention began with a creative choice. Creative choices are not safe, they are not comfortable, and they do not get a lot of support from others (who do not understand them).

Notes:
Our entire lives are actually a complex construction of choices. We make choices all the time about what to think, feel, say, and do. And yet we almost never think deeply about our choices or what a choice actually is or how it works.

Review Chapter 4

Take the chapter review quiz.

Quiz 4.1 - Choice.

Question 1 of 4

What is choice?

A. A Number Of Things To Choose From

B. A Mental (or thinking) Process

C. Possibilities

Question 2 of 4

What is the Power of choice?

A. A privilege for superiors and people with authority.

B. A benefit of having money and power.

C. The mental ability to choose what we think, feel, and do.

Question 3 of 4

The power of choice is also known as...?

A. Chance

B. Will or Willpower

C. Liberty

Question 4 of 4

What types of choices are there?

A. Personal and Business Choices

B. Love and Relationship Choices

C. All of the Above

D. Belief and Creative Choices

Chapter 5
Power

"The primary cause of unhappiness is never the situation but your thoughts about it."

~ Eckhart Tolle

We use a great power when we make choices. We are each born with a divine power to control and manage our reality - the power of choice. Everything we experience is caused by and a direct result of our choices. Everything. The power of choice gives us the power to act in a particular way, direct or influence the behavior of others, and change the course our lives. This is awesome power, and each one of us has it.

Having the power of choice means each of us alone is responsible for the choices we make. The choices we make in any moment affect what we do, everything and everyone around us, and they set the course for our future.

With the power of choice we also get the gift of eternal forgiveness. Eternal forgiveness is the ability to change our mind and make different choices anytime. What a divine design this is. No matter what choice we make in one moment we are always free to make another choice at some other time. This means we can test our choices, see if they are working for us, and change them if we want to. This incredible power to change our mind and make different choices is what is meant by the term eternal forgiveness.

Notes:
We live blindly when we do not take time to understand the awesome power of choice, how to use it, and how it affects our lives.

Review Chapter 5

Take the chapter review quiz.

Quiz 5.1 - Power.

Question 1 of 2

Everything we experience is caused by, and a result of...?

A. Fate

B. Destiny

C. Luck

D. Our Choices

Question 2 of 2

Who or what is responsible for your choices?

A. The Situation or Circumstances

B. YouAre

C. The Person Giving The Orders

D. The Rules and The Law

Chapter 6

Summary

We live free using our power of choice. Each of us alone is completely and solely responsible for our choices. We express our choices as actions, and our actions define us. Our beliefs determine what choices we feel we have. When you feel like you're not free, when you don't have the choices you want, look at the choices you've made and the beliefs you hold. Check your choices and beliefs to see if they are effective for you now. Ask yourself: Are the beliefs I hold and the choices I am making helping me be who I want to be? Are they helping me get what I want? If not, consider changing them.

If we look more deeply at our freedom and our choices, we will see that the changes we want in our life require us to make different choices. The power of choice is the soul of freedom. So choose carefully. Choose wisely. And always be grateful for your freedom - your power to choose.

Notes:

We live blindly when we do not take time to understand our core beliefs and the awesome power of choice each of us has. We live better when we understand how our beliefs and power of choice affect our lives, and how to use them.

Chapter 7

Practice

"Practice makes perfect."

~ Unknown Wise Person

It is one thing to want to change and improve yourself. It is another thing entirely to make those changes.

True and lasting personal change requires consistent practice of new thinking and new actions. Consistent practice transforms what you practice from something new and different into familiar habits. When you think and do different things you have new experiences. Our beliefs, and the habits we develop based on them, prevent us from truly looking at things differently.

Habit Reactions

You develop Habit Reactions to most things. A habit reaction is what you do almost immediately and automatically when a trigger event happens without any thought. Notice that habit reactions are not what you think, they are what you do, or the action you take. You're asked something or you're in a situation and "Bang" you say or do something in response immediately without thinking. That's a habit reaction. Habit reactions feel "right." You will feel uncomfortable if you don't do, or hold back a habit reaction.

Practice Freedom

Here are two things you can do to practice freedom.

Stop. Don't React.

The next time someone asks you for something, anything, practice not saying or doing the first thing you think to say or do. Stop. Just stop. Do not answer immediately. Say what you have to say to give yourself at least an hour before you respond. Say "Let me get back to you on that." And don't give a specific time when you will get back to them. Then do nothing in that hour related to the ask/issue.

The practice here is to take some time to reflect, feel, and notice what you are thinking and feeling before you respond. This practice will help you:

a. **See your Habit Reactions.** Your habit reactions are the things you say and do automatically when a trigger event happens. A trigger event is something you hear, feel, or otherwise experience. You can recognize your habit reactions.

b. **Think about and examine your Habit Reactions.** Because your habit reactions are habits, you do not know what it feels like to not do what our habit reactions do automatically. Because habit reactions are automatic you don't know or even think about what other options you have. And yes, you do have other options available for every situation you encounter that you simply cannot see and access.

This is a gradual practice. It will take months even years to be able to stop doing what your habit reaction wants you to do. One way to think of it is it took all the years of your life so far to develop your habit reactions, it will take some time to change them. Regular practice is all that is required.

Be Aware Of Your Thoughts & Feelings

Notice how you feel when an ask/issue happens. Notice there's a response you want to make almost immediately, something you want to say or do. And notice what feelings you have, the feelings that appear with your habit reaction almost immediately when the ask/issue happens.

Examine Your Habit Reactions & Your Feelings

Notice what your habit reaction wants you to say or do, stop, write down what you want to say or do, then ask yourself these questions in this order:

1. Why do I want to say or do this?
2. What other things could I could I say or do in response to this?
3. Why don't I want to say or do any of these other things in response to this?

Notice what your habit reaction feels like, ask yourself these questions in this order:

1. Why do I feel this way?
2. What other feelings could I have about this?
3. Why don't I have any of these other feelings about this?

The two freedom practices are "Stop. Don't React." and "Be Aware Of Your Thoughts & Feelings." Consistent use of these two practices will unlock more of your personal freedom in the many everyday situations and encounters you have.

Click the link below to get your copy of the "Practice Freedom Tools" for free:

thepersonalfreedombook.com/practice-freedom-tools

Here's to your freedom!

Chapter 8

Chapter Quiz Answers

Quiz 1.1 - In The Beginning

Question 1 of 3

What is forced upon you when you are a child that tells you how you see the world?

Answer: C

Question 2 of 3

Where do core beliefs come from?

Answer: F

Question 3 of 3

What changes a thought into a belief?

Answer: A

Quiz 2.1 - Beliefs.

Question 1 of 3
A thought...?

Answer: C

Question 2 of 3
What changes a thought into a belief?

Answer: B

Question 3 of 3
What do your beliefs do for you?

Answer: A

Quiz 3.1 - Freedom.

Question 1 of 6
What is Freedom?

Answer: C

Question 2 of 6
What takes your freedom away?

Answer: A

Question 3 of 6
Where do the choices you have come from?

Answer: B

Question 4 of 6

You must always follow a rule or law?

Answer: A

Question 5 of 6

You feel like you are not free when?

Answer: B

Question 6 of 6

How can you have more freedom?

Answer: A

Quiz 4.1 - Choice.

Question 1 of 4

What is choice?

Answer: B

Question 2 of 4

What is the Power of choice?

Answer: C

Question 3 of 4

The power of choice is also known as...?

Answer: B

Question 4 of 4

What types of choices are there?

Answer: D

Quiz 5.1 - Power.

Question 1 of 2

Everything we experience is caused by, and a result of...?

Answer: D

Question 2 of 2

Who or what is responsible for your choices?

Answer: B

About The Author

Edward Phelps is a visionary entrepreneur, author, and spiritual guide. He was born and grew up in New York City. Edward has more than 25 years of award winning experience in advertising, marketing, graphic design, digital marketing, and web design & development.

On a twenty seven year journey of self-discovery seeking to answer the question "who am I?" Edward experienced a miraculous inner transformation that completely changed the course of his life (and cured his fear of heights).

On this journey Edward discovered his deepest fears and ultimately faced them. He researched and studied ancient wisdom and teachings that help us discover our true selves, realize our divine power, develop our unique gifts, and share our best selves with the world.

Along the way he noticed that much of this wisdom is found in books and writings that require college level reading skill, or is taught by "Gurus" at retreats that cost thousands of dollars to attend.

Edward founded Pocket Awareness™ to create and publish wisdom for living that's easy to access, understand, and use. Pocket Awareness™ books use a unique structure that Edward designed to make wisdom that helps people live their best lives available to more people. He calls it "Wisdom for all."

"The Personal Freedom Book" is available in digital formats for Apple iBooks and Kindle on Amazon.com. An audio edition is in production and will be released soon.

Contact Edward at edward@pocketawareness.com to share any thoughts or questions you have.

Here's to your journey!

Get the Practice Freedom Tools Bundle FREE!

Practice is the pathway to mastery.

Click the link below to get your copy of the "Practice Freedom Tools" for free:

thepersonalfreedombook.com/practice-freedom-tools

The Bundle features these Practice Freedom tools:

- Practice Freedom Worksheet
- Practice Freedom Journal

The Bundle is delivered in a ZIP file that includes the two Tools files in these formats for Mac or PC:

Apple Pages (.pages)
Apple Pages 09 (.pages)
Microsoft Word (.docx)
Microsoft Word (.doc)

Thoughts & Observations

www.ingramcontent.com/pod-product-compliance
Lightning Source LLC
LaVergne TN
LVHW051022080826
845145LV00009B/2747

* 9 7 8 1 9 4 4 7 1 8 1 2 1 *